TOBY

The Great Detective

in The Carnival Adventure

TOBY HARRIS

Toby The Great Detective
Copyright © 2021 by Toby Harris

Tellwell Talent
www.tellwell.ca

ISBN
978-0-2288-3809-8 (Hardcover)
978-0-2288-3808-1 (Paperback)

To my "Angel"
Evangeline Aurora Essex
Love, Grandpa

Adventure 1

When Toby was a kitten, he loved to play games with his brothers and sisters, especially hide-and-go-seek. He was the best at finding everybody.

His mother use to read them bedtime stories. His favorite was about three little kittens who had lost their mittens. His mother then asked Toby, "What do you want to be when you grow up?" Toby eagerly replied, "A great detective!"

One day while out for a walk, Toby noticed a large crowd of people standing in a line with their pets. The sign outside read, "Carnival Day: Bring Your Pet."

Toby went inside to look around. Soon, he noticed a little kitten crying under a bench. He scurried over and said, "Hi, my name is Toby. What's your name?"

"My name is Purrfect", replied the kitten, between sobs.

"Why are you crying?" asked Toby.

"I lost my owner", said Purrfect.

My first detective case, Toby thought.

"I can help you find your owner," Toby said. "I was a champ at playing hide-and-go-seek with my siblings as a kitten!"

"How are you going to help me find my owner" asked Purrfect. "There are a lot of owners here."

"I have an idea," said Toby. "Maybe if we revisit all of the places you have been, your owner may be there looking for you."

"Good idea," Purrfect said with happiness in her voice.

"Where to first?" asked Toby.

"The rollercoaster," replied Purrfect.

They arrived at the rollercoaster but did not see Purrfect's owner.

"Let's get on the ride," said Toby, "that way when we reach the top we can look down and see if we can see your owner."

So, they went up and up and up on the rollercoaster, but they didn't have time to look for Purrfect's owner. As soon as the ride reached the top, zoom, down it went, then up again and upside down. Toby held on tight. He thought he was going to fall out.

"That was fun!" yelled Toby. "Where to next?"

"The haunted house," Purrfect replied.

They went into the haunted house to search for Purrfect's, owner. Inside, everything was dark. They heard a lot of creepy noises and lots of screams.

When the ride was over, Toby asked, "Did you see your owner?"

"No," said Purrfect, "I was too scared to look around."

"I know," Toby said with a sigh of relief. "I had my eyes covered the whole time."

Toby's tummy started to rumble.

"I am getting hungry," Toby said. "Let's go find something to eat."

"Okay," said Purrfect.

"Mmmm, something smells good," Toby said with a big sniff, "and it's coming from over there."

Toby and Purrfect came across a pizza shop. They were in luck. Someone had dropped a slice of pizza on the ground.

"Mmmm, my favorite," Toby said, "anchovies."

After they finished eating the pizza, Purrfect started crying.

"What's the matter?" asked Toby.

"It's getting dark and I still haven't found my owner," Purrfect said with sadness in her voice.

"Was there any place else you and your owner went?" Toby asked.

"We stood in a long line and got this red collar," Purrfect said with a small sigh in her voice.

Toby looked at the collar. It had a tag on it.

The tag read, "If found, return to the Lost & Found Center located at the front entrance."

"That's it!" Toby yelped. "Follow me."

They ran to the front entrance and saw a "Lost & Found" sign.

There, standing inside, was a sad little girl, asking if anyone had seen her little kitty. It was Purrfect's owner.

Purrfect was so happy. She ran right to the little girl, jumped up in her arms and showered her with kisses.

Toby smiled as he watched the happy reunion.

Toby gave his friend a wave goodbye and set off to find his next case.

CPSIA information can be obtained at www.ICGtesting.com
Printed in the USA
LVIW012022160221
679321LV00002B/18